Hall of Fame

Sports Illustrated
BASEBALL

Sports Illustrated
BASEBALL

BY THE EDITORS OF
SPORTS ILLUSTRATED

**Illustrations by
Ed Vebell**

J. B. LIPPINCOTT COMPANY
Philadelphia and New York

U.S. Library of Congress Cataloging in Publication Data

Main entry under title:

Sports illustrated baseball.

(Sports illustrated library)
1960 and 1966 editions published under title: Sports illustrated book of baseball.
1. Baseball. I. Vebell, Ed, illus. II. Sports illustrated (Chicago)
GV867.S72   1972   796.3572   77-37610
ISBN-0-397-00857-0
ISBN-0-397-00831-7 (pbk.)

Photographs from Sports Illustrated, © Time Inc.
Cover photograph: Tony Triolo
Page 18: Walter Iooss, Jr.
Page 73: Herb Scharfman

Photographs on pages 8, 26, 35, 42, 54, 61, 74, and 87:
Ed Vebell

Contents

Text Revisions by Roy Blount

Sports Illustrated
BASEBALL

1
Harmon Killebrew on Hitting

THERE are two kinds of hitters in the big leagues today—those who try to overpower the ball and those who merely try to meet the pitch. The power hitter bullets hits through the infield, bounces them off the fences and drops them into the seats. The spray hitter to all fields goes with the pitch as he swings and tries to place the ball where it will fall safely. The hitter who combines power with clever place-hitting is in a class by himself. He is a star.

Early in your baseball career you should evaluate your potentialities. If you're a little fellow like Cesar Tovar or Freddy Patek, you should study the art of hitting to all fields. If you are a big strong muscular fellow like me, you should, of course, use your power to the best advantage—but you should also learn how to place hits.

Most young players take the easy way out. They stay in their power groove. They become pull hitters to left if they are right-handers, to right if they swing from the left side of the plate. They get their quota of long hits, but fielders gang up on them, robbing them of many a blow that would have fallen safe if they had learned how to place the ball more expertly.

So the first rule in hitting is to overcome your tendency to be a one-field hitter. This isn't easy. It takes time, patience, long practice and experience. But it pays off in the end.

Now, let's get down to specifics. It's your turn at bat. The nine guys on the other team have one objective in mind—to get you out, no matter how. That pitcher out there on the mound is your worst enemy. He's got a weapon in his hand—a baseball that he's going to fire at you. He's going to use his power against yours and add something extra, a curve, changes of speed, control and a knowledge of your weaknesses. He knows how to throw curves and sliders, sinkers, knucklers, screwballs. He'll use all kinds of deception to make it hard for you to pick up the pitch as it speeds toward the plate. He may bring his leg up high, like Juan Marichal, so that the ball seems to come out of nowhere. He may rear back like Vida Blue, whose delivery comes at you so fast that you can't pick up the ball until it is almost on you. Or, like Dick Hall, he may swivel around and dip his throwing hand behind his knee, jerking his head and shoulders to confuse you. Or, like Mike Cuellar, he may have so many kinds of curves and so many changes of speed that his pitches play peekaboo with your bat.

Okay, then . . . let's say hitting is tough in the big leagues. But you also have brain power, physical power and good eyes. Little details in a pitcher's delivery may tip you off to what's coming. You may notice that the pitcher is holding the ball across the seams for a fastball, or cocking his wrist for his curve. He may show a little more white on the ball for the curve. Or he may rear back a little farther and show less white for his fastball.

Few pitchers make such mistakes in the big leagues. When they do, the opposing manager, coaches and players catch on.

10

The word gets around and the pitcher doesn't last long in fast company. Pitchers are human; they get careless. You can add hits to your record by being alert at bat.

So the next rule is to watch opposing pitchers closely and make mental notes of their styles of delivery and their faults.

Next in importance is your counterweapon, your bat. The bat is really an extension of your body. It must feel as comfortable in your hands as your own arm feels when you swing. And, by the way, your bat must produce hits or be discarded for another one.

Bats used to be pieces of lumber, like Babe Ruth's 42-ounce bludgeon. In recent years many hitters have used 29-ounce "whiplash" bats in order to exploit the full power of their bodies, getting around on the ball quickly, meeting it on the "meat-part." Little men have driven out long hits with such bats, but they also frequently strike out or pop up. The present trend is toward a somewhat heavier bat. I like a 35-inch bat weighing 33 ounces. It suits my style of hitting because it enables me to wait a little longer as the ball speeds in. I can swing smoothly, pull on inside pitches and stroke through the middle or to right on outside pitches.

I can't tell you how to grip the bat. You must find your own best grip. I grip the bat firmly but not tightly. See Figure 1. If you hold it too tightly you won't get a full swing. Be quick with the bat. Move it where you want it to go with the least resistance.

Figure 1.

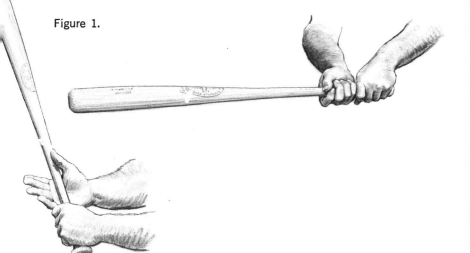

Figure 2.

I normally swing from the handle with the full power of my arms (Figure 2). Some smaller men choke the bat, moving their grip up the handle, to control the direction of the ball. The greatest master of this art was little Nellie Fox, weight 160 pounds, who manipulated his bat for a .298 lifetime average, the hits flying in all directions like popcorn in a frying pan. That's called "bat control."

With your own favorite bat in your hands, step into the batter's box. Keep your eye on the ball from the moment the pitcher takes it from his catcher. If you know pitchers' styles you'll know the approximate area in which he will release it after he goes into his windup. I can pick up a curve as soon as the pitcher lets it go. Fast sliders and fast, sweeping curves usually break late, often right in front of the plate. This is a tough pitch to hit. It takes long experi-

12

ence and perfect timing to connect with a sharp-breaking curve like Andy Messersmith's or Pat Dobson's. But it can be done or they'd pitch no-hitters every time. You can do it if you study pitchers' mannerisms, glue your eye to the ball as it whizzes toward the strike zone and control your bat and do not let it control you.

Figure 3. With proper control of the bat the swing should complete a perfect arc, the hands reversing at its completion.

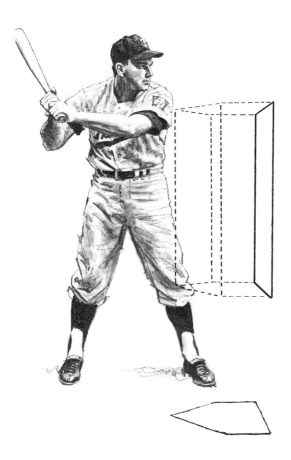

Figure 4. The official strike zone is from the batter's armpits to his knees, but each batter has a strike zone of his own—wherever his bat can reach the ball.

There are three different kinds of strike zones. First is the one in the rule book (Figure 4), which we can disregard because it is just so many words. Second is the umpire's strike zone. Every umpire has one of his own. Umpires correctly gauge the top of the individual batter's strike zone, which varies from batter to batter according to his height or crouch. But umpires have quite different ideas about the bottom of the strike zone. Low pitches at knee level are the

14

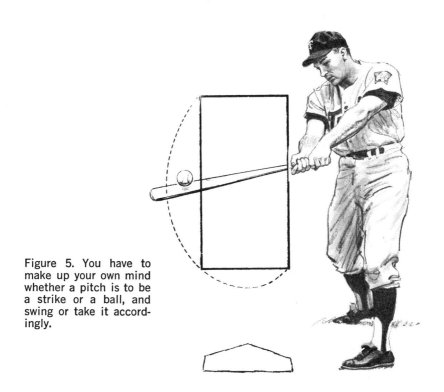

Figure 5. You have to make up your own mind whether a pitch is to be a strike or a ball, and swing or take it accordingly.

hardest to call. There is no use trying to outguess an umpire on low pitches. You have to make up your own mind whether a pitch is to be a strike or a ball and swing or take it accordingly.

This brings me to the third and most important strike zone: the batter's. The batter's strike zone is anywhere within reach of his bat, as you will learn in batting practice and during games. Duke Snider, one of the great hitters of

modern times, went out of his personal strike zone during his early Dodger years. He often struck out, waving futilely at low outside curves. With experience he learned how to lay off such puzzlers. His strikeouts were fewer, his bases on balls more numerous, and his batting average soared. On the other hand, Yogi Berra was a "bad-ball" hitter who often went out of the official strike zone to stroke outside pitches into left field for vital hits, or to pull high pitches to right for home runs.

Your strike zone is as big or as small as you make it, dependent on your ability to connect solidly with the ball.

I take a square, straightaway stance at the plate, my feet parallel to the sidelines of the batter's box. I take a firm grip with the spikes of my left shoe, but I do not dig in like Tony Oliva, who has the ability to use his bat flexibly, hitting to all fields. I am a pull hitter with power to left and left center, and my straightaway stance enables me to come around on the ball in those directions (Figure 6). At times I shift my feet, depending on the pitcher's style, and also when I am trying to hit behind the runner to the opposite field. On this hit-and-run play I close my stance a little, moving my front foot closer to the plate (Figure 7).

16

Figure 6. My square straightaway stance enables me to meet the ball full on at the meat of my bat and get maximum power into my drives.

Figure 7. I am a pull hitter to left and left center but, as the diagrams below show, by shifting my feet I can hit behind the runner to right.

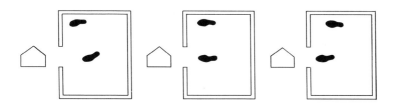

Every batter develops his own natural way of standing up to a pitched ball. I don't believe in changing a batter's stance when he's in a slump. It's a good idea to discuss hitting with your coaches, manager and fellow players. They may notice some little mistake you're making, such as dropping your hands as the ball is delivered. But the best teacher is experience. You yourself must find the batting style that produces the best results—and stick to it.

You should go to the plate confident that you can hit anything the pitcher throws at you. You should observe the pitcher's form and know whether he's getting ahead of the batters or whether he's a little wild. I go to bat looking for the kind of pitch in the area where my power lies. When I'm at the top of my game and hitting well, all pitches look alike to me. If I'm off my game I'm more likely to wait the pitcher out. With two strikes against me I'm ready for anything. I am never tensed up. I am always willing to take a chance on the pitcher's best stuff. The batter who takes a third strike looks foolish. And no wonder—he's let himself be fooled into not swinging.

Your confidence as a batter should be based on the feeling that you can't be fooled by deception because you know the kind of stuff the pitcher uses. Of course, there are pitchers you've never seen before, young pitchers breaking in or newcomers from the other league. But if you study a pitcher's form in the early innings, you should be able to catch up with him on the third or fourth time around. Watch him work on other batters. Get their opinions about him. Many a game has been broken up in late innings by just such analyses of a pitcher's form.

My specialty is hitting for extra bases and home runs. But not everyone is gifted with my physical power. It would be foolish for me and harmful to the team if I changed my style. Nevertheless, I do not despise the shorter hit or even the measly little bunt that trickles a few feet from the plate.

Bunting for a sacrifice or safe hit has won many a game. And many a game has been lost because the batter has been too lazy to learn how to bunt.

To make a sacrifice bunt, square around on both feet as the ball comes to the plate. Move both hands up on the bat, the right hand above the trade mark, the left hand up a little past the handle. Keep your bat in front of your body and on the level. (See Figure 8.) Don't jab at the ball. Give with it as it hits your bat. On contact, pivot and head for first base. (These directions are for a right-hand batter; the position of the hands should be reversed for a lefty.)

The push bunt is a try for a safe hit. The object is to push the ball past the pitcher in the direction of second base. Place your hands the same as for the sacrifice bunt. Instead of giving with the ball, push it as you break for first and then go at top speed.

The drag bunt operation is much like the push bunt except that you try to drag the ball and bat for the first step toward first base, dropping the bat as you get under way.

One of the most difficult bunts to field is the deadfall bunt which bloops a short distance and drops dead. Fielders can gauge a roller by its speed and handle it swiftly, but when the ball has stopped rolling, it must be picked up neatly and thrown from an awkward position. To execute the deadfall bunt, hit down on the ball from above, using your arms to direct the ball either to left or right. A deft bunter with fair speed can upset the whole infield.

The ideal swing for longer hits is one which moves in a smooth arc, meeting the ball on the level—that is, with the bat virtually parallel to the ground as it connects with the ball. To hit a breaking ball low on the outside corner, I use a swing that resembles a tee shot in golf. I put everything I've got into that kind of swing: hips, shoulders, arms, wrists.

In any kind of hitting the hands control the bat. The quicker they are the more drive you get into the ball. Swing the bat through its arc as quickly as possible. Your wrists

Figure 8.

add extra power on the follow-through after you've hit the ball. The wrist snap is that final accelerator after your hips, shoulders, forearms and hands have laid the bat on the ball. The follow-through is proof that you've used every part of your body to get maximum power. A halfhearted swing, the arc cut short on contact, is proof you aren't using all the power you've got. (See Figure 9.)

Figure 9.

On an inside pitch you should get your bat ahead of your hands and your hips out of the way. Jamming is intended to prevent you from pulling the ball. You should stand your ground and not fall back unless the ball is likely to hit you. Never let a pitcher scare you by jamming you high and inside. Be bold. Be brave.

The stride is a vital source of power. My stride is of average length, neither too long nor too short. A batter who hits to all fields may shorten his stride to drive short hits through the infield, then open it up for long hits. Shortening the stride puts more hip action into the ball. A short stride also enables the batter to see the ball better.

In my early days in the big league I had a long and even a wild swing. But for the last half-dozen years I've used a more compact swing and with far better results. In boxing, the short punch is the hardest. That's true of the swing in baseball. It means more hip action and more hits.

Your swing should be the same for a curve as for a fast-ball. The only difference is that you wait a little longer on the curve. The tendency of some batters is to start their swing as soon as they see a curve ball coming. They get their hands ahead of the ball and lose some of their body power. You should keep your hands back and your shoulder up as you stride. Then, at the last second, swing quick, hard and accurately.

To anyone who's never played baseball, hitting looks simple. All you have to do is to swing at a thrown ball and the wood does the rest, as any kid knows. But a big-league hitter must take the art a little more seriously than that.

Pick out a bat which suits you perfectly and stay with it.

Study pitchers, know what their best pitch is, what kind of control they have, and observe their mannerisms so they won't be able to deceive you.

Decide what kind of hitter you are going to be, and once you have adopted a style, stick to it, refining it as you go along.

Whether you're a power-hitting puller or a spray hitter, learn how to bunt and how to hit to the opposite field.

Settle into a comfortable stance and if it isn't bringing results make up your own mind about what's wrong. Listen to advice but don't take it until you know from practical experience that it's right for you. Hit a lot, until you get the feel of your best stroke.

Use a smooth, level swing except on low outside pitches. Try to go with the ball where it's pitched so you won't have an obvious weakness that pitchers will try to exploit.

Take batting practice seriously. Act in the cage the same as you do in a game.

Use the bat as an extension of your arms, wrists and hands. Don't hold it too tightly, or too loosely.

Notice wind direction before and during the game. Notice how the defense plays you and try to find the holes.

Keep swinging at strikes—and lay off bad balls.

Figure 10.

2
Dave McNally
on Pitching

TO GET into pitching to begin with, a young man generally has to be able to throw the ball hard. But to become a pitcher, he has to gain control.

Control means more than just accuracy. Nobody really has "pinpoint control" anyway—you don't try to hit certain spots, you try to get the ball in a certain area in relation to the batter and the plate. Pitching is not like firing a rifle—squinting and setting your sights and just skimming the black edge of the plate. Pitching is a matter of controlling yourself—the concentration of your mind, the coordination of your body—and controlling the situation. Keeping the ball close enough to the hitter's fists, or far enough out away from them, that he can't quite get the leverage he wants. And at the same time staying around the strike zone, so that he can't sit back and wait you out. When the hitters are

27

big-leaguers, all this is about as easy to control as a medium-sized riot. But it can be done.

There is no one delivery that can be prescribed for every pitcher, just as there is no standard batting stance for everyone. Juan Marichal kicks his foot way up in the air and rears back. Some pitchers find they have better control when they take hardly any wind-up at all. The main thing is to find your natural groove, and hope and work to stay in it. Pitching is also like hitting in that a slump is largely a matter of slipping out of that groove, and the best way to get out of a slump is to keep on pitching. A good coach can help detect gross errors, then practice until the right feel comes back. A doctor told me once that the best way for a pitcher to get started off right in the spring would be just to shag flies and throw the ball in naturally, not even thinking about pitching to the plate, and then work up to harder and harder throwing from there.

Certain basic guidelines to an effective delivery can be laid down, however. Here are a few:

(1) The angle of the forearm to the ground as the pitching arm is coming through will vary widely from pitcher to pitcher, and even from pitch to pitch. Straight overhand pitching means the forearm is perpendicular to the ground. "Three-quarters" means the forearm comes through at a 45-degree angle. Sidearm means that the forearm is roughly parallel to the ground. All these different deliveries may be effective. But the upper arm, from elbow to shoulder, should *always* be parallel to the ground as the ball is released. (Figure 11). Try throwing a ball with the upper arm either above or below the horizontal. You just don't get enough power out of your arm that way. Often when I am off my form, it is because I am violating this guideline—temporarily.

(2) The body should stay compact. A lot of flailing around of arms and legs may look imposing, but it is liable to dissipate your power—to let off too much of the steam

Figure 11. As I release the ball I balance my weight on both feet so that I can break in either direction for bunts or topped balls.

that you should be putting behind the ball. Throwing a baseball is like hitting one in that a short, tight stroke is stronger than a long loose one; as in everything else, the less waste motion the better. Watch Marichal or Vida Blue or someone else who has a relatively big motion, and you'll see that all his pumping and kicking is compactly organized —all tightly focused on the job of propelling the ball on its sharpest possible course to the plate.

29

(3) An extension of point (2): don't "open up" too soon. That is, as you stride toward the batter, don't present the front of your pelvis to him too soon. "Opening up" deflects some of your body motion away from the line of the pitch— just as stepping "in the bucket," instead of straight into the pitch, wastes the strength of the batter's hips.

(4) The most important part of your arm action is from the ear forward. You can "reach back for a little extra" for a big pitch sometimes, figuratively, but the extra really comes in as you snap your arm forward a little harder. That's where your speed and your spin is: in that snap forward beginning at about the moment the ball passes your ear. If you start forcing a pitch beginning way back behind your head, you just tighten up and lose leverage.

(5) Always follow through. It's a good idea, whenever possible, to finish up in a good stance for fielding, with your weight evenly balanced so that you can move in either direction after a ball hit back to the box. But an excellent way to guarantee an abundance of balls hit sharply back to the box, or a lot farther than that, is to concentrate so much

30

Figure 12. In this pictorial analysis of my delivery, you can see how muscular control and body coordination help me control the ball.

Figure 13. As you raise your arms for the delivery, conceal the ball in your glove so that the batter cannot see your grip and know what is coming.

Figure 14. The fast ball is gripped tightly and thrown so that it will slide straight off the end of the fingers.

on fielding position that you jerk to a stop, neglecting to follow through. That's where you've got to propel that ball, up front—and if you come to a sudden stop after releasing the ball, it means you've started letting up before you released it.

As I said, the best way to pitch a ball is the way that feels most natural. But it helps if it *looks* a little unnatural. What I mean is, if you're throwing hard, you ought to look like you're throwing easy. The best fastball is one that surprises the hitter, like Blue's. There are other pitchers who throw very hard—Gary Bell was one—but you *know* they're throwing hard, and you swing accordingly. When major-league hitters can get a good fix on a pitch, they're going to hit it pretty consistently—too consistently for the pitcher's good— no matter how much velocity the ball has. By the same token, if you're throwing slow stuff, you need to look like you're throwing hard. Steve Barber used to throw 80 per cent straight change-ups—which meant they weren't changes of pace at all, but his normal pace. And yet the hitters kept missing them. They just couldn't believe that he could throw so hard, apparently, and the ball could come in so slow.

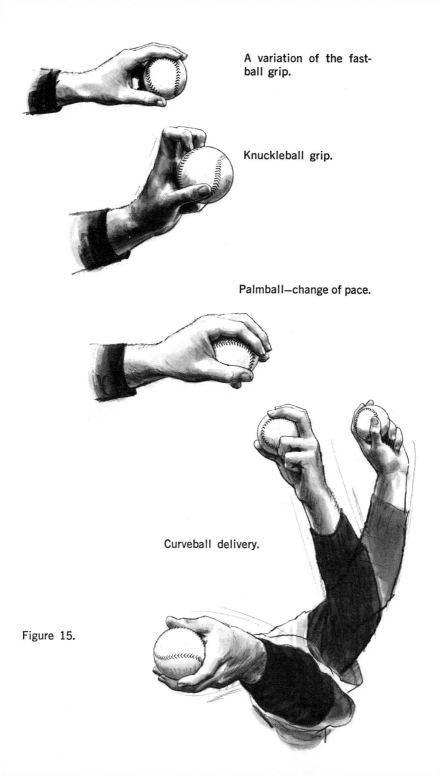

A variation of the fast-ball grip.

Knuckleball grip.

Palmball—change of pace.

Curveball delivery.

Figure 15.

Which brings us to the function of all pitches other than fastballs—"offspeed" pitches, they're called, and they're used to keep the hitter from responding automatically to your pitches with a correctly timed swing. They give him pause, you might say.

The main offspeed pitch is the curve. Not only is it somewhat slower than the fastball, of course, it also has a hook in it. A left-hander's curve breaks away from a left-handed batter and in on a right-handed batter. A right-hander's curve is the opposite. Like a good fastball, a good curve has a tight, humming spin. A curve that rolls in loosely is a curve that hangs—it doesn't break sharply—which is to say that it is highly likely to be hit a long way.

But a curve's spin is different from a fastball's. A fastball is delivered straight off the tips of the first two fingers. A curve is thrown with a snap of the wrist, so that it comes roughly out of the space between the index finger and the thumb. Thus it spins in a different plane from the fastball, and it takes a different flight.

A slider is a sort of cross between the fastball and the curve. It breaks in the same direction as the curve, but it breaks later and not as much. It also comes in with almost as much speed as the fastball. It looks like a fastball— except to hitters who are especially adept at noticing the spin on a ball—until the last moment, when it breaks maybe 6 inches. In throwing a slider, you don't turn your wrist all the way over, as you do when throwing a curve. You just cut the ball slightly as you release it, so that it leaves the fingertips slightly off center. This is an extremely effective pitch—if it breaks. If it doesn't break, it is just a not-quite-so-fast fastball, and one of the easiest pitches to hit.

There are many ways to throw a change of pace. Some pitchers throw a sort of screwball as their let-up pitch. Theoretically, a screwball breaks in the opposite direction from a curve—in throwing it, you twist your wrist in the opposite direction. But hardly anyone throws an actual big-

breaking screwball, such as Christy Mathewson (he called it a "fadeaway") and Carl Hubbell threw in the old days. But when you put that opposite twist on the ball, it does fade away slightly, and it slows down.

A forkball—held in the fork between your first two fingers —is another type of change-up. My change-up, though, is what might be called a palmball. Instead of gripping the ball mainly with my fingers, I hold it way back in the palm, with the fingers wrapped around it. So I throw hard, but the ball comes out dragging.

I don't throw a knuckleball, but Wilbur Wood and Phil Niekro do, and Hoyt Wilhelm broke Cy Young's old lifetime record for number of games pitched in by relying on the knuckler. The pitch is actually not thrown with the knuckles, but with the fingertips dug into the ball and the fingers arched out away from it. As the ball is released, the fingertips are lifted up and the upper pad of the palm pushes the ball toward the plate. This causes the ball to "float" in, with no spin on it. Since it isn't directed by its spin, it follows whatever shifting wind currents may be operating at the moment between the mound and the plate. It may break in any direction, and two or three times. If it doesn't break, though—if the fingers nick it as it leaves the hand, imparting a little spin to it—it is easy to hit.

Those are the offspeed pitches. Remember this: Keep your curve and your slider low. By and large, all pitches should be kept low, but especially the breaking ones. The lower they are within the strike zone, the better they break, and the more likely they are to become nice routine ground balls.

It is also important to conceal from the hitter your intention to throw these pitches. The element of surprise is crucial. So keep your grip concealed by your glove hand.

Now a few words about strategy. You have to know your enemy. You have to know, for instance, *never* to throw a change-up to Tony Oliva. He murders change-ups. And I might as well admit that nothing I throw to Frank Howard stops him. Other pitchers tell me they have good luck against Howard with such and such, and I try it, and he hits it. I'll just have to keep on trying different things until one of us retires.

But in most cases, pitching to a hitter is not a hard-and-fast matter of finding his weakness and avoiding his strengths. Bobby Murcer is a good low-ball hitter, but that doesn't mean that I am going to throw him all high pitches. There are certain hitters, whose names I will not mention, who I know can hit certain pitches—but sometimes, say on a 0 and 2 count, I will throw them the pitch they can hit, and surprise them enough to get them out.

Most hitters are guess hitters. Either they are guessing that you will throw a certain pitch, or they are guessing that you will throw to a certain part of the plate. You try to outguess them. At the same time, you remember cardinal rules: Keep the ball low; don't let the ball get too far out over the plate; stay ahead of the hitter. That last point is especially important. If you get the first strike before the first ball, and stay ahead, then you can call the tune. You can throw pitches that are certainly not too fat and just might be strikes. If you open with a couple of balls, however, the hitter has the edge, because you have to throw pitches that are certainly strikes and just might be too fat.

Before the game you look at the line-up, pick out the big hitters, the ones who are most likely to beat you, and you say, "I am not going to let these guys beat me." These are guys like Harmon Killebrew and Carl Yastrzemski. You are not going to give them anything decent to hit. The other hitters you can be relatively straightforward with—get the ball across with something on it, not too high, not too predictable, and dare them to hit it. Don't walk them so that they'll be on base for the big guns to drive in.

For that matter I never really "waste" a pitch—never throw a ball on purpose, unless I am giving an intentional

Figure 16. I take the sign from the catcher. My weight remains on my back foot until I go into my follow-through.

walk. But when a Killebrew or a Yastrzemski is up, I would rather walk him than give him something he can go to work on. I stay around the edges of the strike zone, maybe a shade outside it. I know that these big hitters are being paid to drive in runs, not to walk, and maybe they will chase a pitch they don't really want if I don't give them anything they do want.

All this, by the way, is up to the pitcher. The catcher gives signs, but they are just so that he'll know what's coming. The pitcher can always keep shaking him off until he comes up with the pitch the pitcher wants to throw. Sometimes a catcher will come to the mound to argue his point, but if the pitcher isn't convinced the catcher has to give in—because unless a pitcher really wants to throw a certain pitch, it isn't going to be a good one.

Checking base runners is important. Supposedly, a left-hander has an advantage in holding a man on first, because he is facing the runner as he winds up. But actually a right-hander is liable to pick more runners off, because the runner can't see what he is doing—and if the right-hander can whirl suddenly to make a move to first, it is very effective. Anyway, even if you can't be a pick-off artist, you have to make sure the runner knows you're watching him, and make sure he comes to a full stop when he leads off. If you let him keep strolling all through your wind-up, he's going to get the jump that you can't let him have. (Sometimes you may just lob one over to first because you didn't have too good a grip on the ball and wanted to get rid of it. Throwing a good pitch, remember, is largely a matter of having the right feel.)

With runners on, you have to make sure you come to a complete stop yourself, at the point when your hands are together at your chest—and any move, even the slightest twitch, that you make after coming to that stop must be the beginning of a delivery. If you twitch in the direction of the plate, you have to throw that way. If you move at all in the direction of first, you have to throw that way. Otherwise, it's a balk.

Whenever there is a runner on with an unoccupied base in front of him, you pitch from a stretch. As a rule you don't stay in the stretch just to hold a runner on third, but you might if he's a threat to steal home and is taking too big a lead for your comfort. Sometimes I've continued to pitch from the stretch with the bases loaded, just because my rhythm was going good that way and I didn't want to change. Anyway you should be able to throw as hard from the stretch as with a full wind-up.

Those are the things a pitcher has to do. If you can do them all with fairly consistent success—and if you hustle

39

and back up the bases on throws, and if you break toward first base on any ball hit to the right side of the infield, so you can cover first if necessary, and if you learn to help yourself at bat by executing the sacrifice bunt and even getting a base hit occasionally—then you are in control of the job of pitching, insofar as anybody can be in control of that difficult job.

Figure 17. Learn the pick-off throw. Set yourself, make a quick step and with the same motion throw to first. Keep base runners on the defensive, especially today when base-stealing is once again popular as an offensive weapon.

3
Brooks Robinson on Infielding

THE MOST intricate, difficult and rewarding maneuver in the infield (spectacular stops aside) is the double play. If the ball is hit to the second baseman the shortstop goes to the bag, takes the throw to force the runner, then pivots and throws to first for the second out. If the grounder goes to the shortstop, then the roles are reversed. The pivot is easier for the shortstop because he comes into the bag moving toward first, while the second baseman almost always is moving away from first. The second baseman should not be in motion as he takes the shortstop's throw. He must run hard until he's 4 or 5 feet from the bag, then jockey in, bouncing from one foot to the other like a boxer, knees bent so he can move to either side for the throw. The shortstop sprints toward the bag, slows as he nears it. When he sees the throw coming in, he sprints again and hits the bag at full speed.

43

If you are playing second the easiest way to pivot is to ease into the bag and straddle it with your right foot—just touching it. Take the throw and make a fast flip to first. As you throw, lift your left foot or leap into the air to avoid the incoming base runner. If the shortstop's throw is to the pitcher's side of the bag, hop to the left toward the mound. If the throw is to the left-field side of the bag, drag your foot over the bag and throw from behind it. You can also come into the base, tagging it with your left foot and edging toward right field as you throw.

As a shortstop, your fastest pivot is by hitting the bag with your right foot and making a fast throw to first, jumping in the air to avoid the runner. The most popular shortstop pivot is to brush the bag with your right foot as you glide across it toward the right-field side, making the throw from outside the baseline. If the throw comes in on the pitcher's side of second, hop to the right, brush the bag with your left foot and throw to first from inside the baseline. Another way is to come in, hit the bag with your left foot and then back off toward left field as you throw to first.

Shortstop's Throw

Shortstops and, for that matter, third basemen, should feed the ball to the second baseman for a pivot with a controlled throw to the pivoter's chest. The ball should come in to the pivoter letters-high so that he can clearly see it. If the shortstop makes the throw close to the second baseman, it should be a lay-up, a simple stiff-wristed underhand toss. There is no single way of throwing to first. Every infielder should learn to throw accurately overhand, sidearm and underhand, depending on the circumstances. If there is time, grip the ball across the seams; a grip parallel to the seams makes the throw tail away or sail, especially on the long throw by the shortstop from the hole or by the third baseman back of his bag.

44

Second Baseman's Throw

If the second baseman is close to the bag he'll use a simple lay-up toss, or half turn and throw sidearm to the shortstop. Beyond 12 feet or more from the bag you should turn and throw with a quick arm flip across your body. When you are in the second-base hole, cock your arm and put more shoulder into the throw. Never grab a ball in the hole to your left and spin all the way around to face second. That's flashy, but you may end up throwing the ball into left field and be the goat of the game.

Third-Base Play

Third base is called the hot corner because you're nearer to that bag than any other infielder. I try to get in front of as many ground balls as possible, in order to knock 'em

Figure 18.

down and throw the runner out. Although some second basemen and shortstops shift positions as much as 20 or 30 feet for certain batters, I rarely shift more than a yard to either side of my normal position. I move back on pull hitters and forward when I expect a bunt. Of course, when my shortstop plays close to second base for left-hand pull hitters like Reggie Jackson or Norm Cash, I'll move over toward the hole.

I take a firm stance, hands on knees, as the ball is delivered. My eyes pick up the ball when it is about halfway to the plate. I am ready to spring into action by the time the ball reaches the plate. (See Figure 18.) I do not commit myself left or right, but I take a short step forward to get a better jump on the ball. By then I am up on my toes, ready to go either way.

The most important detail of infielding is getting your glove right down on the ground as soon as you can. (See Figure 19.) Balls that infielders miss usually go through their legs. The less motion you make, the surer you are that

Figure 19.

Figure 20.

you'll come up with the ball. Remember this—it's easier to go up for a high hop than to go down for a grass cutter. Keep your glove low.

On hard-hit balls to your right along the foul line, pivot on your right foot before grabbing the ball. On hard-hit balls to your left, pivot on your left foot and cross over to the spot where the ball can be fielded. (See Figure 20.) On this kind of drive, it's advisable to veer back at an angle when you pivot, in order to be in a better position for a throw.

The Bunt

The third baseman's toughest play is a bunt. Always nab a bunt with your glove unless it is coming to a stop or has stopped. That's the only time you should use your bare hand. (See Figure 21.) In fielding a bunt use two hands as you

Figure 21.

come in. (See Figure 22.) Take the ball from your glove, take one step on your right foot and you're in a position to throw. Otherwise you'll have to take two steps, one on your left foot, another on your right before throwing, losing a valuable second.

Figure 22.

With none out and runners on first and second, the batter will try to bunt toward third in order to pull the third baseman off the bag. I tell the pitcher to break to his right toward third so that if the ball comes into that area he can field it while I am covering third. Of course, when the ball is bunted up the third-base line I must field it, the shortstop covering third, if possible. On the other side of the diamond the second baseman covers first when the batter bunts up the first-base line. Third and first basemen must make sure that the pitcher can field the ball before they break to their respective bases. Otherwise the bases will be full.

A squeeze play with a runner on third cannot be stopped if the batter bunts effectively, but the pitcher should try to keep the runner close to the bag. The third baseman should play as close to his bag as possible.

The Pop Fly

Knowing which way the wind is blowing is a great help in going after pop-ups, fair or foul. Check wind direction before and during games by looking at the flags on the grandstand roof. Don't drift with the ball and get to the spot just in time to catch it. (See Figure 23.) Get to the spot where you think it will come down, and then wait. On a foul pop-up near the stands, get over to the stands as fast as you can and then dive in after the ball if you have to. If you drift over, you'll find yourself keeping half an eye on the stands and lose the ball. Try to catch pop-ups above your head. This gives you a second chance to catch the ball should you muff it. Willie Mays is the only player I've ever seen make a basket catch consistently at his waist and never drop the ball.

Never yell "I got it!" until the ball has reached its peak. Otherwise it may drift on you and fall safe. On pop fouls the ball has a reverse spin which carries it toward fair territory. If a high foul back of the plate is reversing in flight, you as an infielder have a better chance to catch it than the catcher, who must throw his mask away, turn around, sight

Figure 23.

the ball and then try to get it. Whenever an infielder has as good a chance as the catcher at a pop-up, the infielder should take it.

If you are tall, wiry and agile—and a left-handed thrower —you qualify for the job of playing first base. You need your height and mobility to handle infielders' throws delivered to you from all angles, and your agility to cover the considerable territory within your range, while your left-handedness means that you wear your fielder's glove on your right hand, which enables you to handle ground balls in the fair territory at your right without crossing your arms to get your glove in the way of hot grounders. And power at the bat won't hurt, for most successful first-sackers are long-ball hitters.

Your territory includes the area in which bunts are dropped. Here in reverse you should handle them much as the third baseman does. The same techniques as the third baseman's apply to the handling of pop flies into fair or foul territory in extreme right field. With a runner on first and none or one out, you defend against steals, sacrifices and hit-and-run plays by holding the runner on, playing in front of the bag. You should know the capabilities of the batter in such situations and be prepared for the type of hitting he does best. Experience and/or hard practice will help you acquire that good judgment which makes the first baseman an important defensive unit in a tight infield, especially in knowing when to go after ground balls and when to let another fielder get them while you cover your bag.

The old idea that the first baseman is merely a target for throws is dead today. The polished operator at this vital position (1) snuffs out runners at second, third and the plate with quick, accurate throws, (2) teams with the second baseman in covering the hole into right field, (3) whips the ball to third or the plate on bunts or infield taps and (4) is the anchorman who keeps the entire infield steady.

Baseball is a game of team play and team play is at its

best in a crack infield. Each infielder is a member of a team within the team. Learn to work with your pitcher, catcher and fellow infielders and you'll help win many a game.

4
Tim McCarver on Catching

THE BACKBONE of a ball club is the line from catcher through the mound and second base to center field. The catcher is at the base of this line. He is the most active player on defense. All the action lies in front of him. He can check the defensive alignment and rearrange it to suit the situation from play to play.

The catcher is the team's thinking apparatus. Watch a catcher when things get tough. He puts on his thinking cap and walks around in a little circle, calculating, figuring, making a decision which may be the difference between victory and defeat. With a glance over his shoulder he can pick up a sign from his bench manager. With a glance to his left he can steal a sign from the other team's third-base coach.

His head is a filing cabinet where all sorts of information about the other team's players and strategy is stored. A

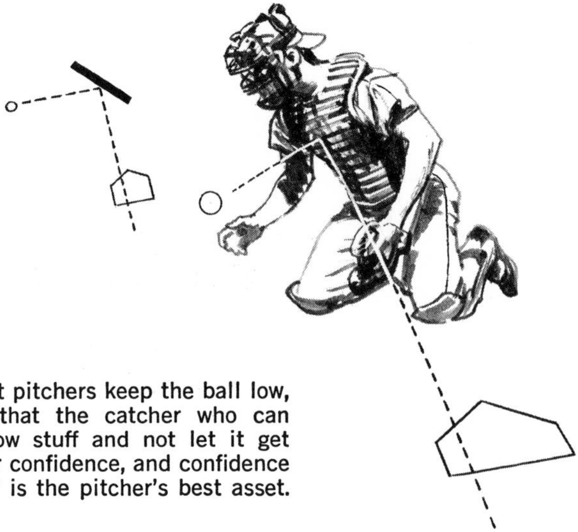

Figure 24. Most pitchers keep the ball low, which means that the catcher who can handle their low stuff and not let it get away wins their confidence, and confidence plus good stuff is the pitcher's best asset.

catcher is a walking encyclopedia of facts about the hitting habits of every player in the league.

The pitcher is usually the key man in any game, but pitchers will tell you that the catcher can be equally important in controlling the trend of a game.

The catcher should know the stuff and both the mental and the physical condition of every pitcher on the staff. Is your pitcher getting off the beam, missing corners, throwing too high? Is he pitching too quickly? Is he getting upset? It's the catcher's job to know and to do something about it, slowing him down by holding onto the ball between pitches or, if necessary, firing him up by calling time and going out to talk to him. A kind word or a wisecrack or a little needling can revive a sagging pitcher sometimes.

Ideally, the pitcher and catcher should work together in harmony, thinking alike and agreeing on how to pitch to the various batters. The unity of the entire ball club depends on the batterymen's relations with each other. I think it's as important for the catcher to know his pitcher as for him to know the strength and weakness of the opposing batters.

The catcher must be the teacher, friend and guide of rookie pitchers. The pitching coach may tell a youngster *how* to pitch but the catcher is right there on the field while the rookie *is* pitching. He can detect faults and correct them on the spot. He can cure the rookie's jitters with a few calm words. He can say, "Forget that it's Willie Stargell up there at the plate. Just pitch to him as though he were Joe Zilch, batting .147. Give him your best stuff, and you'll get him out."

Catching is hard work, but it's also great fun, for you're running the game. And you get to know the game far better than you ever thought you could. Your memory knows. When a batter has socked a home run off one of my pitchers I can remember what kind of pitch it was two years later. All major-league catchers can. But you double-check that kind of information at pregame clubhouse meetings or in private talks with your pitchers.

Don't set up pitching patterns. Opposing managers and coaches get wise to such patterns and relay the information to their hitters. Each time at bat is a new experience. Your judgment will tell you what to do in any given situation. When I'm in a tough spot, 3 and 2 and men on base, it's my policy to call for the pitcher's best stuff, because on the average the pitcher has the advantage over the batter. It's proven by statistics that good pitching gets the good hitters out. Very few hitters finish the season with an average as high as .333 nowadays—and that's only one hit in three times at bat. Don't call for pitches that you think will outsmart the hitter. The smarter way is to pit strength against strength, call for the pitcher's best.

I agree with what Bill Dickey used to say: A catcher should be the pitching staff's best friend on and off the field. Personality conflicts aside, you should work and live as closely as possible with your battery partners. It pays off in mutual confidence, and confidence wins ball games.

The catcher is the team leader, the guy who shovels the coal into the boiler that makes the engine go. It's not a lazy man's job.

The first thing the catcher does before each play is to go into his crouch. There is no standard crouch. My advice is to crouch in the way that is most comfortable for you. Get comfortable. Relax. Distribute your weight evenly. I shift to my right side when I see a runner taking a long lead off base, so that I'll be in a throwing position as quickly as possible. (See Figure 25.)

Now that you're settled in your crouch and on your toes for quick action, give the sign. I put my mitt over my left knee to conceal the sign from the hitter and his third-base coach. I set my right knee a little in front of my left knee to conceal the sign from the first-base coach.

Make your signs as simple as possible. Don't confuse your pitcher by changing signs when a runner on second is in a position to see the sign you are calling. Few base runners try to steal signs these days. It isn't a profitable business, for the runner must relay the sign to the batter and the batter must take it and then hit. The batter is better off when he's on his own, using his own best judgment about what kind of pitch is coming up.

After giving the sign for the next pitch with one or more

Figure 25. Be prepared to catch the ball with your hands well in front of your body. Distribute your weight evenly. In this way you will be able to move easily in any direction to catch or block the pitch.

fingers, I show a hand sign to indicate whether I want it high, low, inside or outside. A closed fist, an open palm, a hand laid on the inside of the left or right thigh conveys that sort of information. (See Figure 26.)

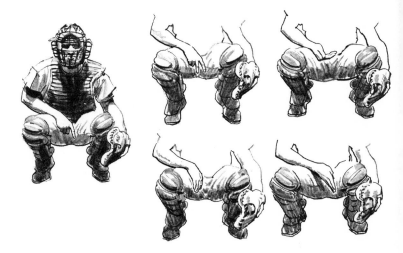

Figure 26. Make your signs as simple as possible. I put my mitt over my left knee to conceal the sign from the hitter and his third-base base coach. I show a hand sign to indicate whether I want the ball to be high, low, inside or outside.

Next, set the target for your pitcher. This can be done solely with the glove or by combining the glove's position with a slight shift of your body to left or right. (See Figure 27.) Don't worry about tipping off the batter with your body shift. He's too busy figuring out how to hit the next pitch to pay attention to your changed position.

Unless a pitcher is hopelessly wild he's going to place his pitch approximately where you have called for it. When a curve is coming, you must anticipate its hitting the dirt. Be

Figure 27.

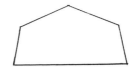

ready to block the ball. Block it with any part of your body so that it will bounce in front of you.

I think a real good fastball is much harder to catch than a curve (Figure 28). Bob Gibson's fastball moves tremendously. Sometimes it takes off to one side or the other, and sometimes it's as straight as a string. When I was catching him I had to react quickly or it might get away from me.

Some catchers call for a fastball when a runner is in a

Figure 28.

stealing situation. I don't. I concentrate on the hitter as if no one was on base. If a fast curve or a knuckler is likely to fool the batter, call it. If you call for a fastball and it's hit out of the park, you won't have a chance to throw the runner out. No matter how fast the runner may be, don't let him influence your judgment about the man at the plate.

The bugaboo of all catchers is the knuckler. Not even the pitcher knows what his knuckler will do. He doesn't throw it to a point in the strike zone. He throws it to an area. Remember this: When you are catching a knuckleball, stay relaxed. Be prepared to grab the ball at the last second by being free and easy, able to move in any direction. When you get the ball, squeeze it. It's got a mind of its own and may pop out of your mitt.

Catch the ball as far in front of your body as possible without interfering with the batter. Umpires are fooled sometimes by curve balls which break out of the strike zone after crossing the plate. You are not trying to trick them by grabbing the ball before it goes outside. I never try to jerk a ball back into strike territory after catching it. I catch the ball in front of me to make sure that the umpire calls a legitimate strike.

The catcher controls a bunt situation even if he is not involved in handling the ball after it has been bunted. With a runner on first, or runners on first and second with none or one out, the catcher must anticipate a bunt. In any bunt situation, come up from your crouch as the ball is pitched. (See Figure 29.) Don't be lazy with men on—split seconds count. Be ready to get out of the chute and into play. But don't move up from your normal position before the ball reaches the plate. The batter may swing, and, if he does, your mask may come into contact with his bat and he'll be awarded first on an interference call. Be ready to move either way to field the bunt. If the ball falls outside your territory and must be handled by another player, yell to the player nearest to it, the pitcher, the third baseman or the first

Figure 29.

Figure 30. Using your glove as a broom to sweep the ball into your throwing hand is a timesaver that may help retire the bunter or cut down the runner when he is trying to advance on a sacrifice.

baseman. Yell to which base the ball should be thrown.

On bunts rolling dead, use your glove as a broom to sweep the ball into your throwing hand. (See Figure 30.) This is another trick that saves valuable time.

In bunt situations, with men on first and second, keep in mind the relative speed of the men on base. (See Figure 31.) There's no time to think after the ball has been bunted. You should be able to judge by the placement of the bunt and the runners' relative speeds whether a throw will get the lead man or whether you should throw the bunter out at first.

Figure 31. On balls poked to your left a bare-hand pickup helps in making a quicker throw to first.

Blocking low pitches in the dirt is one of the catcher's most important duties. Put both knees to the ground, your glove in the middle, your bare hand in your crotch area and behind your glove so that it won't be hit by the ball. (See Figure 32.) On wide outside pitches don't shift your body. Go after them with your glove. You just can't move your body that quickly.

On all throws to base, throw overhand, even on pick-off tries. (See Figure 33.) The only exception is when you field

Figure 32. Curves break low. When they hit the dirt be prepared to block them. If the ball hits in front of you and bounces up, your body will stop it from going through for a wild pitch or a passed ball.

Figure 33.

Figure 34. Throw your mask away as far as possible when you go after a pop-up. Keep your hands high for the catch.

a bunt while off balance and must throw sidearm or underhand to save time. Try to grip the ball across the seams. Otherwise you may throw a sinker that will be tough for the infielder to handle. The overhand throw should be timed so that on an attempted steal it will sink naturally at the spot where the base runner is sliding into the bag. Keep the throw at the infielder's waist level so that it won't bounce into the dirt.

The catcher is in charge of all pop-ups in the vicinity of the plate, both in fair territory and foul. It's a good idea to know exactly how much territory you must cover in the sector behind the plate so that you can get to any point without crashing into the stands.

First locate the ball. Then throw your mask as far as possible so you won't stumble on it. Be relaxed. Don't scramble. Remember that most of the time a foul pop-up has a reverse spin and will arch toward you as you go after it. (See Figure 34.) The same applies to balls popped up in front of the plate. When the ball is hit high enough, be ready to spring in any direction if it should be caught in a wind current. Go forward first, then turn, then come back in as the ball falls. Most of the time an incoming infielder will be in a better position to catch a pop-up than you. But be prepared—you may have to take it yourself. If you can't get to it, yell to an infielder who can.

The catcher should offer a stone-wall defense against incoming runners trying to score. Let's suppose the batter hits a long fly ball with a runner on third. The catch is made, the runner tags up. The throw comes in, either in the air or on a bounce. As soon as you catch it you have the right to block the runner, but not before. You should hold the ball in your bare hand. Otherwise the runner will try to knock or kick it out of your glove.

The catcher must be alert from the first pitch to the last in every game. He must be ready for any emergency, he must store all kinds of little facts and a few tricks in his head. He can't pitch for the pitcher, but he can make him pitch better than he thinks he can. With a bunt sign on, he must make the pitcher come in high with a fastball, the hardest kind to lay down. Even when a runner like Lou Brock is stealing, the catcher must throw unhurriedly, accurately and high enough for the ball to be handled easily and yet not so high that it will wind up in center field.

The catcher must know when and when not to use the pitch-out, and never to use it until after the batter has taken one strike. With the count two balls and one strike, that's the time to keep one eye on the runner, another on the batter and—if only you had three eyes—on the pitch that's whizzing to the plate. That's the best time to use the pitch-out, the time when the runner is most likely to take off for second base.

Or take this situation: Men on first and third and the man on first taking off. You've got to throw to second, of course; but before you do, fake a throw to third or just glare that man on third down before you throw.

You've got to be rugged to be a catcher. You've got to take mashed fingers and raw hands. You've got to wear all that equipment when the temperature's hitting 90. You've got to be thinking like mad from first to last.

But it's a great position to play. The catcher is the manager of his team on the field, the guy who makes the wheels go round!

5

Tommie Agee on Outfielding and Base-Running

THE OUTFIELDER has a lot of ground to cover, and he is a long way from the men he has to get out. He usually makes fewer and simpler (which doesn't necessarily mean easier) plays than the infielder, but he is expected to make far fewer errors. If an infielder lets a ball get by him, there is an outfielder backing him up. If an outfielder fails to stop one—well, it sometimes takes a while to catch a bouncing ball from behind. To defend all that open space out there, the outfielder must have speed, a knack for judging the flight of a long ball quickly, and a strong, accurate arm. (See Figure 35.) And he has to be able to figure all the angles.

I've played all three outfield positions in the big leagues, and actually centerfield is the easiest for me, because a ball

Figure 35. The outfielder should have a strong and accurate arm. His judgment about where and how to throw is vital. He is the key man on cut-offs and relays.

hit to center seldom hooks or slices, and is less likely to get lost in the lights. Center is a responsible position, though, because the centerfielder has to range furthest, and he is the captain of the outfield. He usually calls out who is to catch any fly in the outfield—whether the shortstop, the second baseman, the left-fielder or the right-fielder—and he should catch any ball himself that he can. So whenever he decides a ball is his, the centerfielder has the right to call off any

other fielder. He should do this by yelling, "I got it!" loud
enough to be convincing—and the fielder who has been
called off should yell, "Take it!" in the same way. An
accident like the winter-league collision between Rico Carty
and Matty Alou, in which Carty smashed his knee so badly
that he missed the whole 1971 season, just shouldn't happen.

The centerfielder must have an outstanding arm because
he has the deepest field, but the right-fielder's throw to

third base demands an especially good arm too. It is particularly important for a centerfielder to know how to play the hitters, because he has two gaps—left center and right center—to protect, and the other outfielders usually key on him in stationing themselves. But all outfielders have the important obligation of being in the right place at the right time.

Of course you never know for sure where a hitter is going to hit a particular pitch, but by using your head you can cut way down on the chances of a ball's coming down where you aren't. As a rule, hitters pull the ball—a right-handed hitter will hit to left and vice-versa. But that doesn't mean outfielders just swing a few steps toward left against any right-handed hitter and stay there until a left-handed hitter comes up. Take a man like Pete Rose, who sprays the ball in every direction, whether he's batting left- or right-handed. You have to play him more or less straightaway—except when he has two strikes. Like Tony Perez, Rose will go to the opposite field after his second strike, so you shift and play him more or less as though he were batting from the other side.

Your pitcher makes a difference too. Henry Aaron is a great right-handed pull-hitter, but against Tom Seaver he tends to go to right field. Generally, right-handed hitters pull more against left-handers—but when Jerry Koosman is throwing his real good fastball, they won't be pulling him much. If your pitcher relies upon offspeed stuff, he will be pulled more. If he throws hard but is beginning to tire, hitters will start getting around on his fastball, and you had better be ready for some pull-hitting. You can't ignore factors like these and expect to compensate by running hard after the ball. You have to plan ahead *and* run hard.

The outfielder must think in advance of every play. He must know the score, the inning, the number of men on base, and the number of outs. With the score tied in the ninth, two out and a man on first, an extra-base hit may score the winning run. Therefore you must play deeper than usual to cut off any long drive before it falls safe. With the score tied in the ninth and a man on second, you must play shallower to catch a line drive or a short fly, or to throw to the plate if a ground ball goes through the infield.

The outfielder should be able to handle a ground ball with an infielder's smoothness and speed. On artificial turf, the ball is liable to come at you as fast as it comes at infielders on grass. With none on base, I charge in for a ground-ball single, slowing up as I approach the ball, getting down on one knee to block it, my glove in front of my body to make sure that the ball won't go through my legs. (See Figure 36.) Slow up as you approach a shot through the infield or you may let the runner take an extra base.

Figure 36. As you charge in for a ground ball, get down on one knee to block it. Put your glove in front of your body to make sure that the ball won't go through your legs. If the ball bounces up it will strike your body and bounce in front of you where you can pick it up.

When a runner is on second, in easy scoring position, I run at full speed to the ground ball, meanwhile judging by the ball's speed whether I have any chance of retiring the runner on a throw to the plate. If I think I can make the throw I complete the motion of fielding by coming up in a throwing position. (See Figure 37.) But if the hit is dying into a slow roller on the grass, I get down on one knee, conceding the score but keeping the hitter from stretching his single into a two-base hit.

Figure 37.

When you're new in the league the good runners will take chances against you, going for the extra base, and then you've got to throw them out to make them respect your arm. Once that respect is established, however, runners will be more cautious, and the idea is to keep them that way. When a great runner like Lou Brock is taking his turn, you want to concentrate on coming up with the ball quickly and getting it back in to the infield. Don't loaf and give him an excuse to challenge you. When Brock challenges you, it's because he knows you can get him only with a perfect throw, and perfect throws aren't common.

The outfielder should check wind direction before and throughout the game. He should know how air currents in the various parks affect balls hit in the air.

He should be able to break in any direction for a fly ball, aiming for the general area first. (See Figure 38.) It's best to keep your eye on the ball all the way, but sometimes you

Figure 38.

have to turn your back to it and tear off to where you think it's going to come down. Then, just before you reach that point, you look up over your shoulder and try to find the ball again. If you see that you've turned the wrong way, that the ball is going to come down on your other side, don't try to switch around and look over the other shoulder. That means losing sight of the ball again, and it'll be too late to pick it up again. Just keep looking at it and continue to turn in the same direction, until you've made a full circle and come around to the ball. If you have time after catching up with the ball, slow down and plant yourself under it with your arms up, so that you'll catch it high. The closer to your eyes the ball comes down, the better chance you have of catching and holding it. That's if you're a normal outfielder. If you're another Willie Mays, you'll want to catch the ball below your waist. But nobody has been another Willie Mays yet.

The best outfielders, particularly centerfielders, play shallow—except against long-ball guys like Aaron and Willie Stargell. The average hitter's chances of getting the ball over my head are a lot less than his chances of dropping a hit between me and the infield.

You've got to get a jump on the ball. Just as in stealing a base, the first three or four steps are the most important. Try to get down as low as you can, with your feet firmly planted—for the same reason that a sprinter crouches down and puts his feet on blocks at the start. I can tell that I'm getting a good jump on the ball when I find myself breaking in one direction or other on a ball that is fouled back—I am already moving in the direction the hitter is swinging his bat, before he touches the ball. (See Figure 39.)

The outfielder also must make quick decisions on whether to dive for a sinking line drive or a Texas leaguer, or play it safe and cut the ball off on the hop. I won't dive for a ball unless I get the sense as I run after it that it's going to hit my glove. But the game situation makes a big difference.

84

Figure 39.

Both of the diving catches I made in the 1969 World Series came with two outs, and with two men on base one time and three the other. With two outs, the runners were going, and if the ball hit the ground they would probably all score anyway. When there's no tomorrow, you dive as hard as you can today.

When a ball goes into the left-center or right-center "alley" for extra bases, the outfielder nearest the ball should handle it. The other outfielder should yell where to throw it. If a runner is trying for third, the backer-upper should yell, "Third!" And so on. The same applies to the situation where a relay to the plate is necessary. The backer-upper should yell, "Cut-off-man! Cut-off-man!" The head cut-off man will be either in right center or left center, holding up his glove and yelling for the ball. Keep relay throws up in the air; they're easier to catch.

One of the cut-off men is called the "trailer." If the ball has been hit to right he's the shortstop. If it's to left, he's the second baseman. In each case he trails his pivot partner by about 15 feet, so that if the outfielder throws the ball over the head cut-off man's head, the trailer will take it and complete the relay.

Every outfielder should consider himself an extra infielder. He should be prepared to back up the infielder in front of his territory in case a ground ball goes through or takes a bad hop. Start in at three-quarter gait on every ball hit to the infield. You may stop the hitter from taking that extra base.

In a sacrifice situation, the centerfielder should back up second base in case the ball is thrown there and gets through the infielder covering that bag. If you are playing left field and the sacrifice is intended to move a runner to third, back up the third baseman. On a sacrifice bunt toward first, the left-fielder should angle over to prevent a possible throw by the first baseman from getting loose in left center.

Running the Bases

I'm a free-swinging hitter, so I don't get as good a start going from home to first as a spray hitter with a short, controlled swing does. Anyway the idea is to take a quick short step with your back foot, straighten yourself out as quickly as you can and then go. If I'm trying to beat out an infield hit, I run straight at the base. (See Figure 40.) If I'm running out a ball hit to the outfield, I always take a turn at first—even if it looks like no more than a single, you never know when the fielder's going to bobble the ball. In order to get my momentum going toward second, I swing out as much as five yards to the right of first, then come hard through the bag. Turning, I hit the inside of the base, ideally with my left foot—that saves a step—but it's better to hit it with the right on a natural stride than to lunge with the left. If the ball is behind me in right field, I listen to the first-base coach. If I can see the ball, it's up to me to decide whether to go for another base. If I feel that the fielder's got to make a throw right on the bag to get me at second, then the percentages are on my side and I ought to go for it.

If I have to stop at first, I start watching the pitcher and looking for a chance to steal. I have to take a lead that I know I can get back from. I used to take only the length of my body, but now I go out a little farther. There are one or two pitchers in the league, though—Juan Marichal, Phil Niekro—that you can't even take the length of your body on, they've got such deadly moves to first base. I call such a move a balk, but the umpires don't agree.

Here are some tips about leads off first:

(1) Never cross your left foot over your right foot or you will be more vulnerable to a pick-off. Edge off, body facing the pitcher. On your first step off first, put your left foot slightly in back of your right foot. Let your left foot take over. (See Figure 41.)

Figure 40.

Figure 41.

(2) To get the earliest possible jump, study the pitcher and figure out the earliest possible giveaway that he is going to throw to the plate. (See Figure 42.) Some pitchers—but not many anymore—use the same rhythm on every pitch, so that you can time them and break on the count of three or something. By and large, you watch a left-hander's shoulder and a right-hander's foot for signs of commitment to the plate. If a left-hander's shoulder starts toward you,

Figure 42. In stealing, it's the first spurt forward that counts. The time to steal is when the pitcher is going into his delivery. Watch his front shoulder as it dips back or down or when he aims his lead foot toward the plate.

Figure 43.

you know he's got to throw toward you, or balk; and if his shoulder moves toward the plate, he's got to throw that way, and you can go. It's the same with a right-hander's foot—except that with Marichal and Niekro, it's awful hard to tell which direction that foot is pointing. You always steal a base on the pitcher—the best catcher in the world can't throw you out if the pitcher lets you get those first few steps soon enough. You don't steal bases on sheer speed either. Willie Davis has always been one of the fastest men in baseball, but he was around for several years before he learned to study the pitchers and steal.

(3) On a pick-off throw intended to keep you close to the bag, take a couple of steps and touch the bag, moving away from the tag. When you're too far off base and the pitcher has a good movement, dive headfirst to the bag, putting your hand on its outside corner. (See Figure 43.) The first baseman will be tagging at your hand, so it doesn't make much difference where you fling your body. If he tries to tag your body, your hand will already be on the bag and the umpire will call you safe.

(4) As you break for second, bring your left foot over your right foot. If you take the first step with your right foot you won't break in a wide stride; you'll lose the step which may be the difference between stealing the base and being thrown out.

On the hit-and-run, I don't wait for the ball to be hit, I just try to steal the base. If the batter hits a line drive that is caught, I'm going to be doubled off anyway; if he swings and misses I may get the steal; if he hits a ground ball I'll probably make it to second and avoid the double play; and if he hits a single I should make it to third or even go all the way around.

(5) When you're stealing, try to run on a pitch that isn't likely to be a pitch-out—preferably, wait until the pitcher is behind the batter and can't afford another ball. If you should get caught in a run-down between first and second,

try to work your way toward second and hope for a high throw. But if you get out of a run-down, you're lucky. If you're caught between second and third or third and home, and there are runners behind you, try to prolong the run-down until they can advance.

When it comes time to slide, I seem to get to the base faster if I go headfirst. But not too many people slide head-first; just the crazy ones. Not many people use the old Ty Cobb hook or fadeaway slide anymore either, where you swing wide and catch the corner of the base with your foot. Sometimes I'll slide past the base to one side and catch it with my hand as I go by. That's a Maury Wills slide. Usually the best slide is straight-in, feet first, hitting the bag and bouncing up immediately. (See Figure 44.) Slide on your rear end as much as you can, to avoid hurting your legs.

Figure 44. The good base runner bounces up immediately, ready to take advantage of any slip by his opponents. He should have only one idea in his head—how to move on to the next base.

(6) When you're being forced at second and the second baseman or shortstop is pivoting to throw to first for a double play, you're supposed to make it hard for him. Knock him off balance, keep him from throwing the ball— just as long as you're going toward the base, you're not guilty of interference.

When you're trying to score on a ball in motion, the catcher will either be in front of the plate or up the baseline looking for a throw. You have the right-of-way until he has the ball in his hand. When he is in possession of the ball he has the right to block you. If you have to go into him, always do it feet first, and aim for his shinguards with your cleats. That way, as few people as possible get hurt.